A TOY

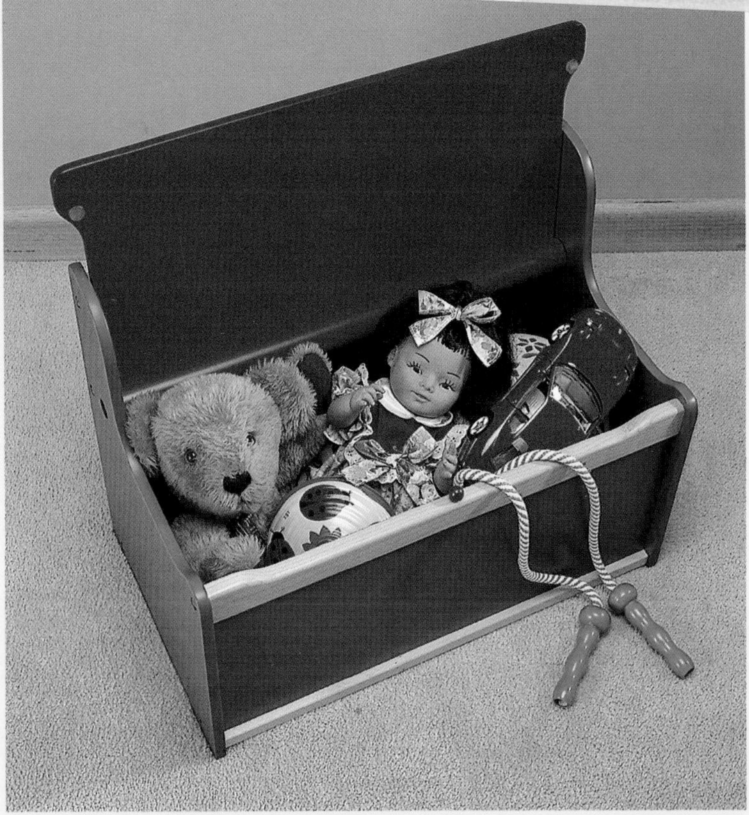

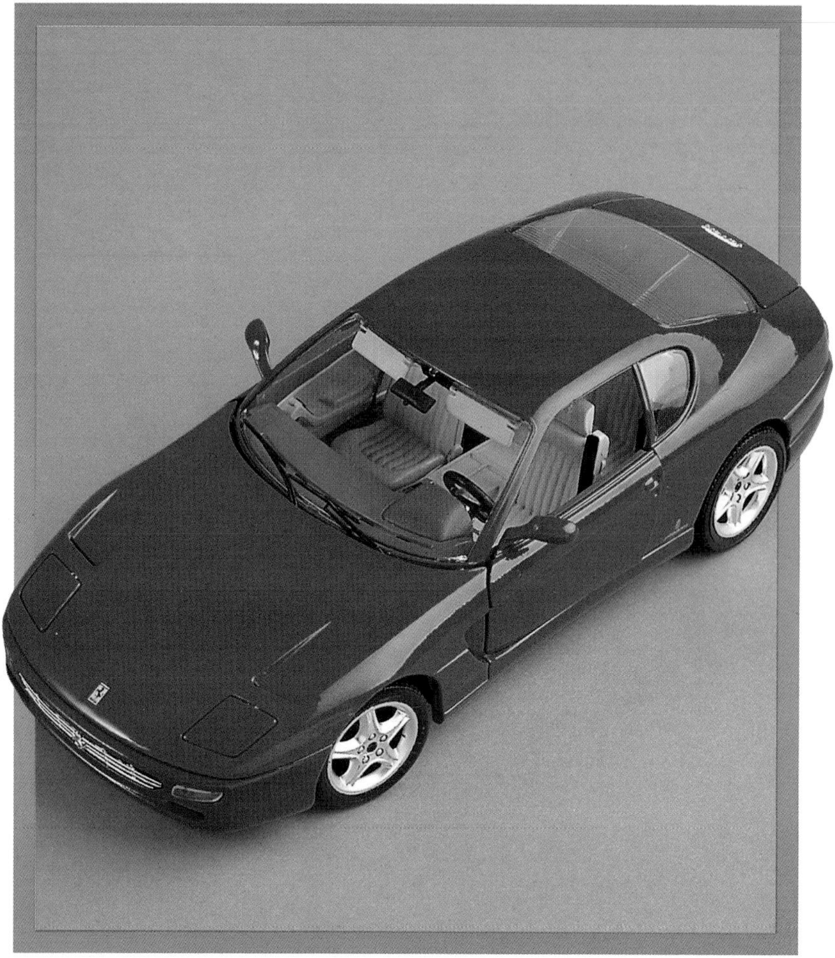

A car,

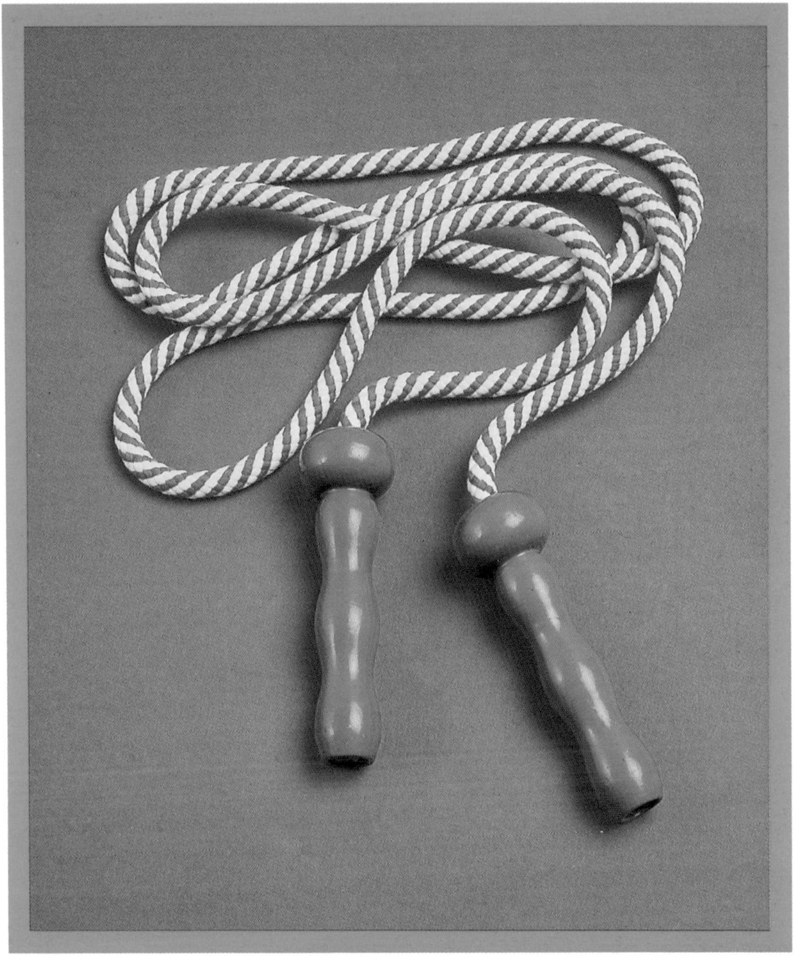

a jump rope,

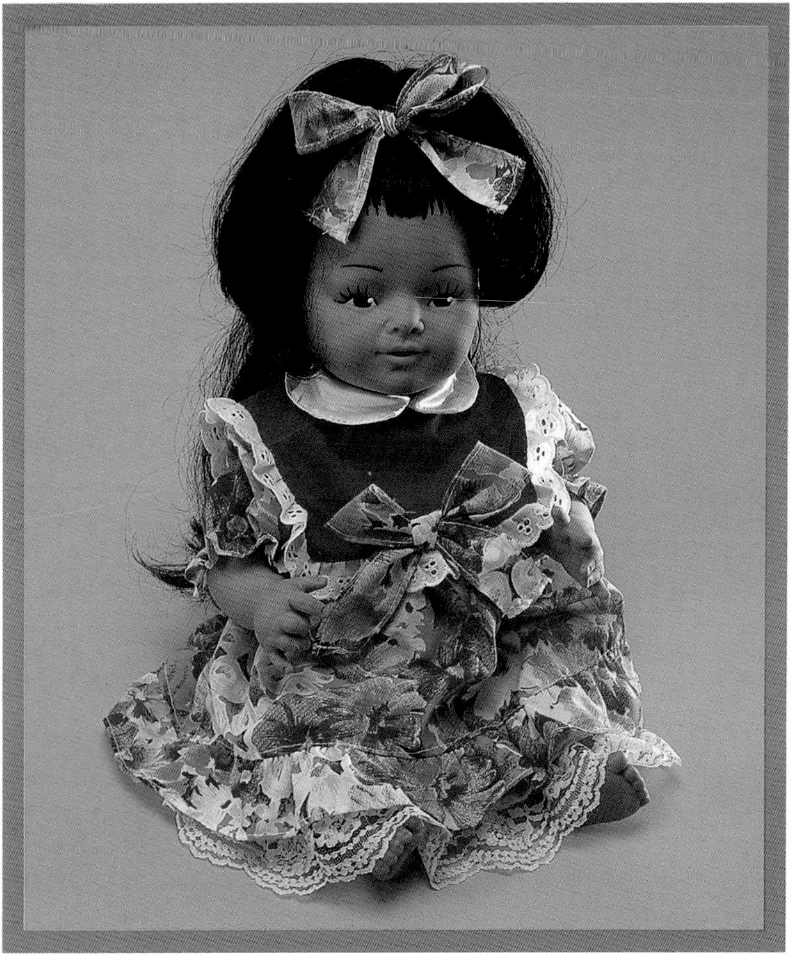

a doll,

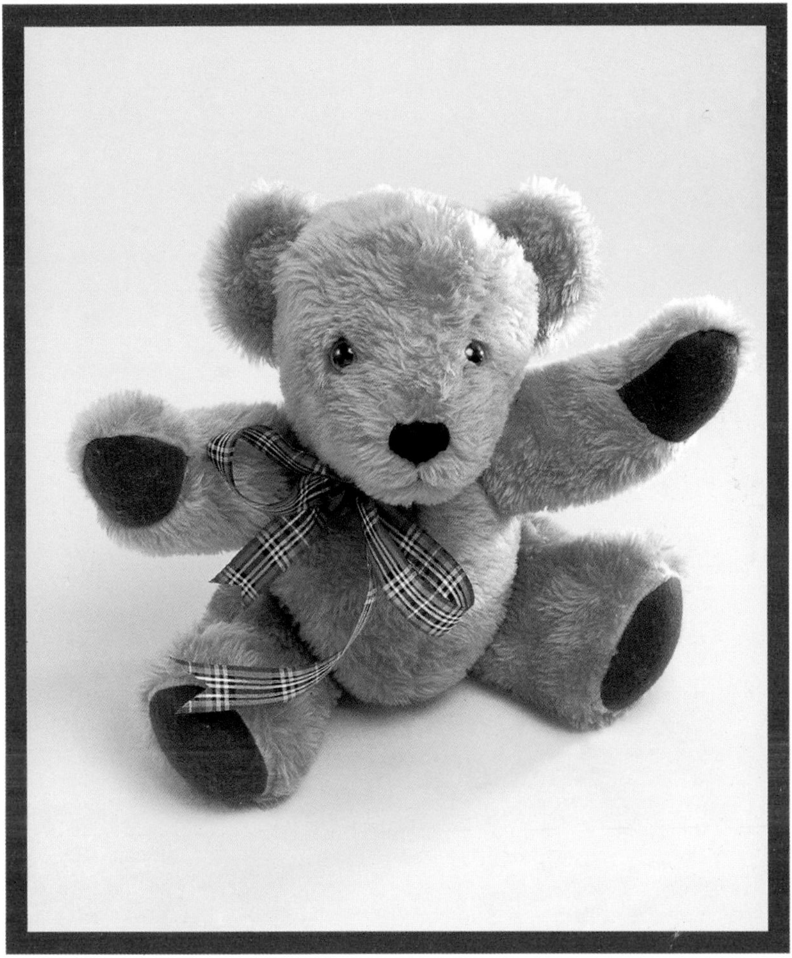

a teddy bear,

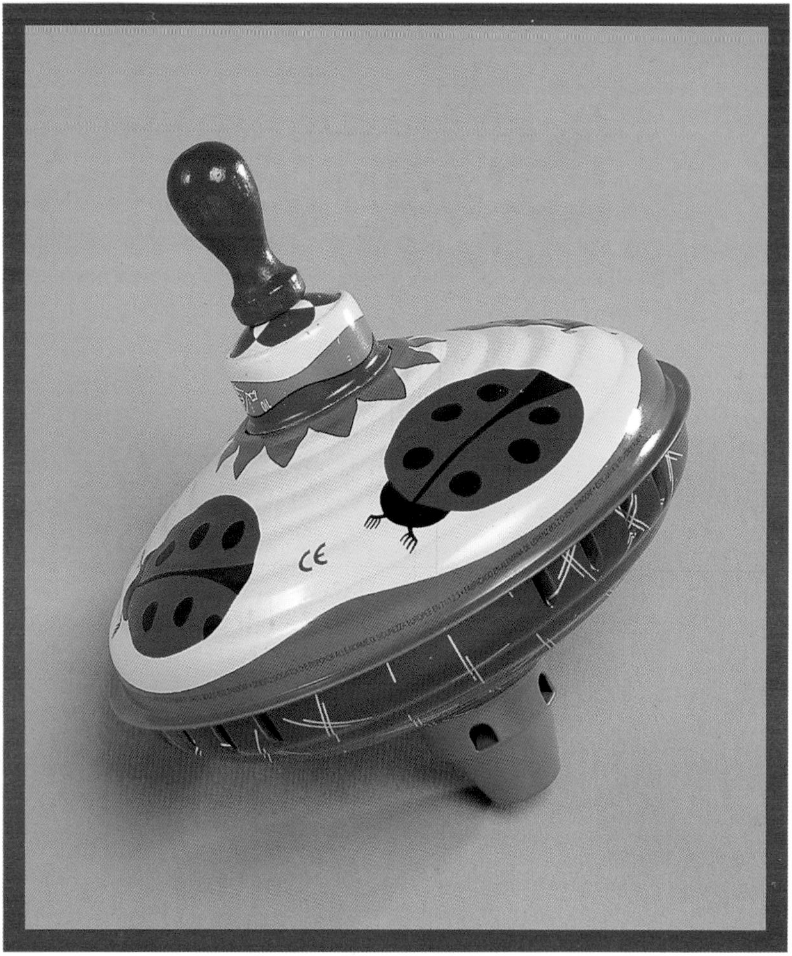

a top,

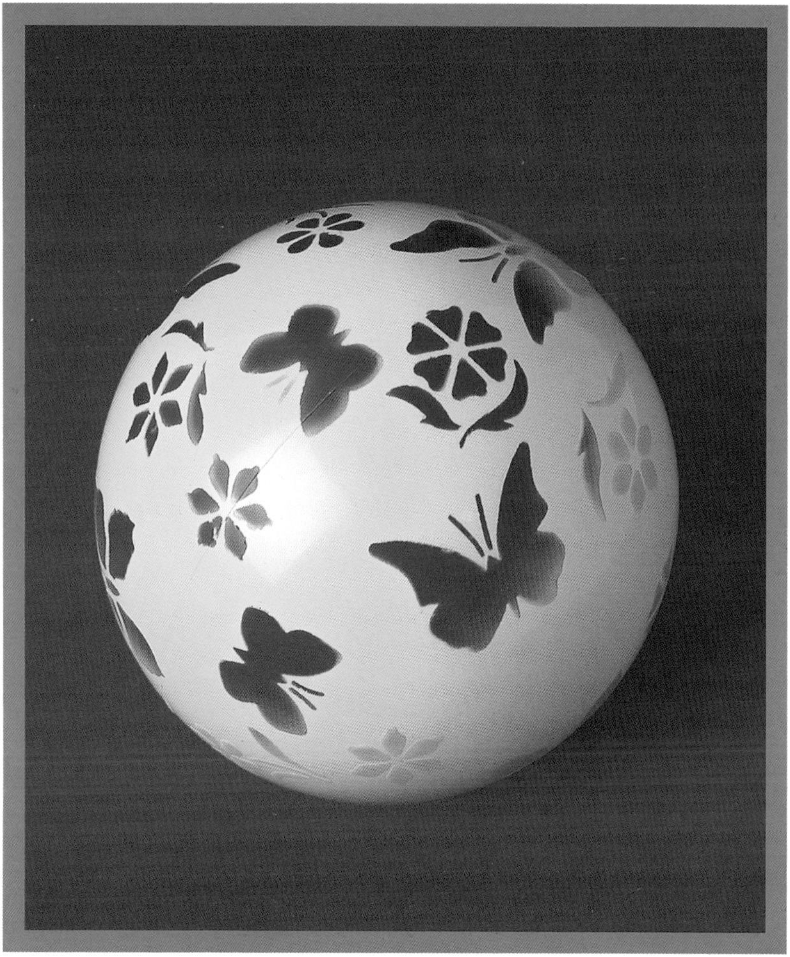

a ball...

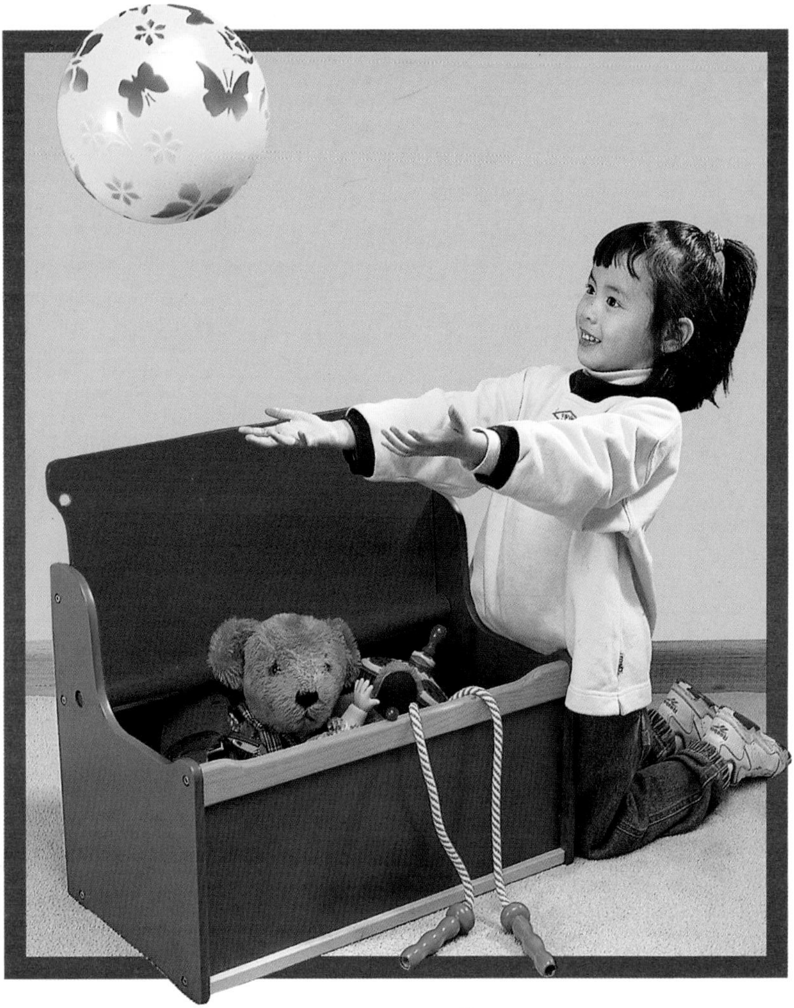

a toy box.